John Butterworth

Illustrations by Jocelyn Wild

(Student's Book)

OXFORD UNIVERSITY PRESS

Introduction

Using The Oxford School Dictionary is a stimulating book of exercises and games to be used alongside *The Oxford School Dictionary*. The book has two parts:

Part one, *Using The Dictionary*, provides a basic guide to the workings of *The Oxford School Dictionary*, and encourages its use as a source of not only information but also of pleasure and amusement.

Part two, *Exploring Language*, contains activities that broaden into a series of language themes, such as the origins of English, the way its words are formed and used, and how they change and evolve. In the process, some strong cross-curricular links are established with history, geography, technology, science, maths, and modern languages.

Using The Oxford School Dictionary is targeted at Key Stage 3, and within this band offers a wide range of tasks and challenges. Whilst the language level, especially in Part two, is sufficiently demanding to extend the students' vocabulary and linguistic experience to the full, the activities can be approached in a great variety of ways to suit wide-ranging needs. Practically all the questions and assignments lend themselves to discussion prior to (or in place of) written answers; and many teachers will want to use the activities this way, so that students can benefit from each other's ideas, working – and playing the games – together.

Using The Oxford School Dictionary satisfies requirements in all five attainment targets of the National Curriculum, approximately between levels 4 and 8 inclusive. Some of the statements of attainment are addressed directly in the subject matter: amongst them, AT1 6(d), AT2 5(d), AT4/5 7(a). Others are encountered less directly, as a product of the activity: contributing to a discussion (AT1), improving spelling (AT4), or turning to other reference materials to pursue an enquiry (AT2).

Contents

Part one Using the Dictionary

Dictionary Quiz	2
Entries	3
Order	4
Discussion and Group Work	5
What it Means	6
Numbered Entries	7
Words in Use	8
Word-Stairs *a game*	9
Word Classes	10
Duffinitions *a game*	12
Singular and Plural	13
Verb Forms	14
Derivatives	16
Pronunciation	17
Phrases	18
Usage	19
Connections *a game*	20
Origins	21
Appendices	22
Acrostic Definitions	23

Part two Exploring Language

Synonyms	24
What Kind / What Difference?	25
Opposites	26
Word Associations	27
Male and Female	28
Compound Words	29
Prefixes	30
Suffixes	31
Roots	32
Word Stems	34
Inflexions	35
The Origins of English	36
How Words Develop	37
Language Groups	38
Old English	40
Middle English	42
Latin	44
Greek	46
Science and Technology	47
Word Travels *a game*	48
Nouns and Pronouns	50
He, She, It or They? *a quiz*	51
Adjectives	52
Complements *a game*	54
Adverbs	55
Actions	56
Feelings	57
True or False? *a quiz*	58
What's the Connection? *a quiz*	59
New Words	60

Part one **Using the Dictionary**

Dictionary Quiz

What can you find out from a dictionary?
Use your copy of *The Oxford School Dictionary* to answer the questions in the quiz.

1. What is **saffron** used for in cooking?
2. What language does the word **safari** come from?
3. What do the letters of the word **derv** stand for?
4. Whereabouts is an animal's **hock**?
5. Around what date is the winter **solstice**?
6. What does an **osteopath** do for a living?
7. Would you be wise to drink something **noxious**?
8. What colours are the flowers on a **magnolia** tree?
9. What do the two halves of the word **dinosaur** mean, and what ancient language do they come from?
10. How many players can take part in a game of **mah-jong**?
11. Where does a **Catherine wheel** get its name?
12. In the word **longevity**, how is the *g* pronounced?
    i as in *long* ii as in *orange*.
13. Which word is incorrectly used in the sentence:
    'Good food will insure good health'? What is the correct word?
14. What is the connection between the month of **September** and the number **seven**?
15. What name is given to the people of:
    i **Finland** ii **Ghana** iii **Cyprus**?

Discussion

Who was James Watt and what does the dictionary tell you about him?

Why do you think Watt's name is mentioned in the dictionary? Are all famous people included? If not, try to find the names of some who are included and think of some others who are left out.

Entries

Each word in the dictionary and the information given with it is called an **entry**. Here is a typical entry, with its parts labelled:

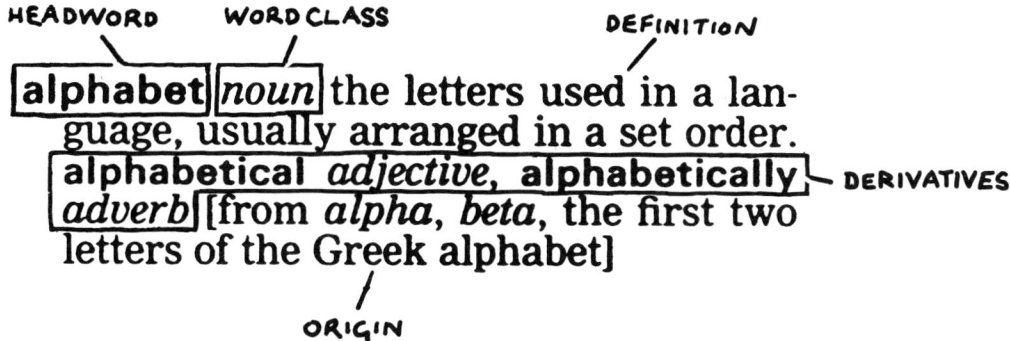

1. Which part of the entry tells you what the headword means?
   Which part of the entry tells you what sort of word the headword is?
   Which part of the entry tells you where the word came from?
   Which part of the entry lists some other words which are close to the headword in spelling and meaning, but are used in different ways?

2. Copy and label the following entries:

   concussion   **dynamic**   **tempt**

Discussion

Do all entries contain the same amount of information?
Look at, and discuss, these entries in particular:

desiccated   **onlooker**   **tubular**
graze *verb*   **helix**   **compulsory**

Erdor
Order

Can you see what is special about the letters of the word **begin**? The letters are in alphabetical order:

a **b** c d **e** f g **h** **i** j k l m **n** o p r s t u v w x y z

1. If you rearrange the following groups of letters into alphabetical order, they will each spell an English word.

   wonk   stif   nich   thogs   potad   scocta

   Work out what the six words are then write them down in an alphabetical list.

   With the help of a dictionary, find **five** more words whose letters are in alphabetical order.

2. The headwords in a dictionary are in alphabetical order, to make them easier to find.

   Sort the following sets of words into the order in which you would find them in the dictionary.

   motion   mystery   meeting   mutiny   maximum

   pleasure   parade   punctual   predict   poetry

   slow   slender   sleepy   slippery   slack

   these   theirs   they   them   then

3. What do you notice about the order of the words in the next sentence?

   Animals cannot easily escape from the zoo.

   Can you make up any similar ones?

Discussion and Group Work

1. If you look in the Yellow Pages of the telephone directory, you will find that many businesses have names like:

   ABC Taxis   Abacus Computers   Baa-baa Wool Suppliers

   The idea is to be near to the top of the alphabetical list. Why, do you think?

   Using the dictionary, invent a clever, catchy name for each of the following kinds of business. It should be near the beginning of the alphabet.

   a pet shop   a health food restaurant   a mobile disco

   Working as a group, put all the names you have thought up into an alphabetical list, as they would appear in the telephone directory.

2. One of the disadvantages of an alphabetical dictionary is the difficulty in finding a word when you don't yet know how to spell it.

   For example, imagine you had just heard these two words for the first time:

   hygiene   hijack

   How many different spellings might you try before you find them?

   i Discuss, and make a list of, the most problematic letters in the English alphabet; and of some words that are difficult to find until you know the right spelling. You could test their difficulty by saying them aloud and asking other people to look them up.

   ii Can you think of any other system by which words could be stored and found? What would be the advantages and disadvantages of your system?

Library Assignment

Find and list some other books, besides dictionaries, which have lots of entries in a certain order. Is the order always alphabetical?

What it Means

One of the main functions of a dictionary is to give the meanings of words. In most entries this information is provided by the part called the **definition**. For example:

lifeboat *noun* a boat for rescuing people at sea.

A definition has to be exact. It must give the full meaning of the headword.

1 Write a short definition of your own for each of the words below. Then look in the dictionary and compare its definition with yours.

mainland   obstacle   conquer   fish   seven   grey

Revise and rewrite your definition if you think it needs improvement.

2 Many words have more than one meaning. When this is so, the definitions are numbered, as they are in this entry:

judge *noun* 1 a person appointed to hear cases in a lawcourt and decide what should be done. 2 a person deciding who has won a contest or competition, or the value or quality of something.

Look up the following words and count the number of separate definitions each one has.

harsh   dry *(adjective)* **abuse** *(verb)* **explode   follow   out**

Discussion

Look up these five words:

do   go   to   after   some

How do you think they and their meanings are different from most other English words? Can you think of a few other examples to add to the list?

Numbered Entries

mail¹ *noun* letters or parcels etc. sent by post.

mail² *noun* armour made of metal rings joined together, *a suit of chain-mail*.

These are not two definitions for the same word. **mail**¹ and **mail**² are entirely different words that happen to be spelt in the same way.

Words like these are called *homographs*, and are shown by the small numbers immediately after the headword.

1. Look up **homograph** in the dictionary. What does the dictionary give as an example of a homograph? How is a *homograph* different from a *homophone*?

2. Look up the following homographs. How many different entry numbers are there for each one?

   bass   batten   bay   fell   felt   fast   sound   lay

3. Here are some words with short definitions next to them. Are they different definitions for the same word, or are the words homographs? (If they are homographs, the dictionary will give them separate, numbered entries.)

   overdo do something too much
   overdo cook food for too long

   deal a bargain or agreement
   deal a kind of wood

   hover wait about, linger
   hover hang in the air

   hind at the back
   hind a female deer

   date a certain day
   date an arrangement to meet

Words in Use

The meaning of a word is not always clear from the definition alone. It is often helpful to see how a word is used in a sentence or phrase.

In the following entry there is an example of the headword in use; it is printed in *italics*.

continual *adjective* continuing for a long time without stopping or with only short breaks, *Stop this continual quarrelling!* **continually** *adverb*.

1 Look up these words in the dictionary and write the example or examples that are given for them.

definite   **makeshift**   **other** *adjective*   **virtual**   **zoom**

Why do some entries need more than one example?

2 Here are several words, each with a definition. Try to write examples - phrases or short sentences - which make these meanings clear. Then compare your examples with the ones given in the dictionary.

absent *adjective* not here; not present

flow *verb* gush out

maul *verb* injure by handling or clawing

offend *verb* do wrong

deluge *noun* something coming in great numbers

Word-Stairs
A game for two or more players

    TABLE
        BLESSING
              INGREDIENT
                      ENT...

Each stair is formed by taking the last three letters of a word and using them as the first three letters of a new word.

How far can you continue the stairs without repeating any of the words? You can use the dictionary to help you.

Make *word-stairs* into a game using sheets of squared paper, each with a *starting line* drawn five columns from the left, and a *finishing line* five lines from the right. You will need around twenty columns in between - more when you become expert.

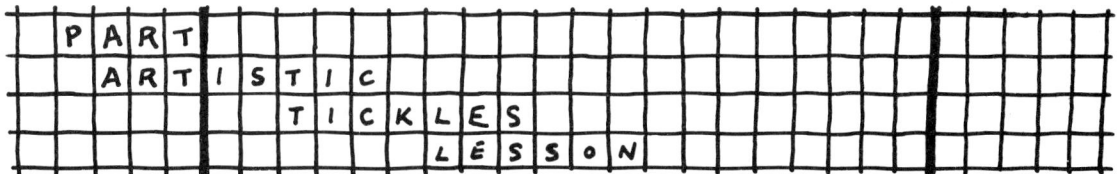

To begin with each player chooses a word of four or five letters and writes it behind the starting line. On the word 'go' the players construct *word-stairs* as fast as they can. The first across the finishing line is the winner.

No word may be used more than once.

Only dictionary words count; use the dictionary as the 'referee'.

Word Classes

As you have probably noticed, every headword in the dictionary is followed by one of these words in italics:

noun   pronoun   adjective   verb   adverb

preposition   conjunction   interjection   abbreviation   prefix

These are called **word classes** or **parts of speech**. They tell you what kind of word the headword is and how it can be used in a sentence.

1 Look up the following words and write down the word class each one belongs to:

   old   ocean   often   operate   or   oh   OPEC

2 Which word class do these belong to?

   horse   hospital   hockey   helicopter   hill

3 And these?

   come   carry   calculate   choose   chew

Word classes are the name for *sets* of words. Here is a set of adjectives:

   good   green   glossy   gloomy   gigantic

4 Write out a set of:

   i five *adjectives* beginning with **r**
   ii five *adverbs* beginning with **s**
   iii five *nouns* beginning with **t**

A word can belong to more than one class.

cheat *verb* **1** trick or deceive somebody. **2** try to do well in an examination or game etc. by breaking the rules.

cheat *noun* a person who cheats.

The headword appears twice in the entry, once as a verb and once as a noun.

5 Look up the following words and note how many different word classes each one belongs to.

lift   limit   little   light¹   light²

6 This is a *Venn diagram*. It shows words belonging to one, two, or three classes.

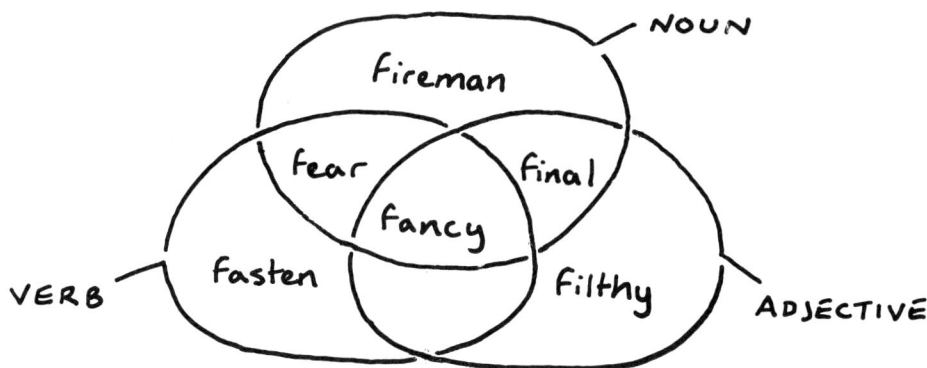

From the diagram:
  i pick out a word which can only be a *noun*
  ii pick out a word which can be a *noun* or a *verb*
  iii pick out a word which can be a *noun* or a *verb* or an *adjective*

7 Draw a Venn diagram and place these words on it correctly, after looking them up in the dictionary:

open   paint   create   cold   double   eyesight   imaginary

8 How many word classes do each of these words belong to, and which classes are they?

home   test   sound   east   run

Duffinitions
A game for two or more players

What is the correct definition of the following word?

myriad (*say* mirri-ad)

- i an adjective meaning innumerable, too many to count
- ii a noun meaning a shiny metal that reflects light
- iii a verb meaning show surprise or amazement.

Two of the choices are *duffinitions*: they are completely wrong. If you don't know the word, **myriad**, have a guess at its meaning and then use the dictionary to see if you are right.

You can play *Duffinitions* between teams of three or four, but it requires some preparation.

With the help of the dictionary, each member of the team writes down a word that no one else is likely to know, along with one proper definition. The others in the team write a *duffinition* for it. Obviously, you must keep your preparations secret.

The idea of the game is to challenge the opposing team to pick the correct definition from the three or four alternatives that you read to them. If they choose the true definition, they score a point; if they don't, you score.

Singular and Plural

Nouns are words which stand for things.

Most nouns have two forms: *singular* when they stand for one thing, *plural* when they stand for two or more.

1. Sort these nouns into two sets, singular and plural:

   town   river   horses   girl   friend   shoes

   nose   cradle   engines   computer   politicians

   How can you tell the singular and plural forms apart?

   Which forms of these nouns does the dictionary give: singular, plural, or both?

2. Write down the plural forms of the following nouns:

   church   ferry   calf   wife   spy   tooth

   potato   helix   child   aircraft   formula   fish

   Which forms of these nouns does the dictionary give - singular, plural, or both - and why?

3. What is unusual about the following nouns? (See if you can work out the answer before looking the words up in the dictionary.)

   scissors   trousers   bellows   graffiti   gymnastics   data

4. Sort these words into singular and plural nouns:

   dahlia   criteria   media   fuchsia   bacteria

Discussion

If a witch's recipe said, 'add four sheep's eyes to the potion . . .' how many eyes would you add - four or eight?

If, instead, the recipe said 'add four pig's trotters . . .' how many trotters would you need?

What have these questions got to do with singular and plural nouns?

Verb Forms

Verbs come in a number of different forms.

Look up the verb **break**. It gives four forms: the headword and three in brackets.

break *verb* (**broke, broken, breaking**) 1 divide or fall into pieces ...

1 Write four short sentences, showing how the different forms of **break** can be used.

Which of your sentences are in the *past tense* (about something that has happened at an earlier time)?

2 The usual, or *regular*, way to form the past tense of a verb is to add the letters **-ed**.

happen > happened

Look up **happen**. Its **-ed** and **-ing** forms are not spelt out because they are regular: they follow the rules exactly.

Write the **-ed** and **-ing** forms of these regular verbs:

call   stay   work   express   intend

3 The following verbs are also regular, but adding **-ed** or **-ing** causes slight changes to the spelling. Write the **-ed** and **-ing** forms, and then check them in the dictionary.

explode   stop   plan   cry   compel

4 These next verbs are *irregular*: they have different rules. Write down their past tense and **-ing** forms and then check them in the dictionary.

come   run   weep   sleep   fight

5 Do the same with these, which are a mixture of regular and irregular verbs.

benefit   bring   commit   limit   manage

Which are the regular ones?

As well as an ordinary past tense, some verbs have a special form for use in sentences like this one:

    She has **broken** her promise.

It is called the *past participle*.

1. Use the dictionary to find out the past tense and the past participle of these verbs:

eat   wake   write   speak   do

2. Take the ten verb forms you collected in question one and write an example of the way each one is used. The example should be a short but complete sentence. Examples:

    Who broke this window?
    You have broken your promise.

3. The **-ing** form of a verb is called the *present participle*. Write five short sentences containing the present participles of each of these verbs:

flap   ski   reply   shine   damage

4. Try looking up the verb **grew** in the dictionary. You won't find it unless you look under **grow**.

Under which headword must you look to find the following verbs?

thought   challenged   won   smiling   risen

Derive
Derivatives

A derivative is a word which comes from another word, usually with some small change to its spelling or pronunciation. For example:

conjure *verb* (**conjured, conjuring**) perform puzzling tricks
    conjuror *noun*

Conjuror is a *derivative* of **conjure**.

Also look up **report** and **reporter**.

1 Write two sentences, one giving an example of how the verb **conjure** (or **conjured**) is used and the other giving an example of how the noun **conjuror** is used. Do the same for **report** and **reporter**.

2 What do you call someone who does each of the following?

cycles   instructs   invents   grumbles   grovels   competes

corresponds   represents   applies (for a job)   **enters** (a race)

3 The word in brackets does not fit the following sentence, but one of its derivatives does. Which one?

Tomorrow is expected to start [**fog**].

The answer, of course, is **foggy**.

i Which derivative of the word in brackets is needed to correct each of the following sentences?

The weather did not spoil the [**magnificent**] of the occasion.
Many children were [**orphan**] by the earthquake.
That is [**total**] the wrong [**explain**].
The expedition came [**perilous**] close to disaster.
The event was of great [**history**] [**important**].
There has been a sharp [**intensify**] of [**hostile**].
New members have to attend an [**initiate**] ceremony.

ii Make a table showing the word class of each of the words in brackets and the word class of the derivative you replaced it with. Example:

fog *noun* > **foggy** *adjective*

Pronunciation

The work on this page needs to be done in pairs or small groups.

Before starting, read and discuss the notes about pronunciation in the front of the dictionary.

1. Taking turns, say each of the following words aloud, whilst your partner checks in the dictionary that you have pronounced it correctly.

   You may well have to look at the list of sounds in the front of the dictionary as well as the entry itself.

   fuselage   **connive**   **house** *verb*   **grotesque**   **bass**[1]

   depleted   **excerpt**   **intrigue**   **hectare**   **maelstrom**

   prestige   **hypothesis**   **vociferous**   **fluorescent**   **sceptic**

   prologue   **viscous**   **ricochet**   **visage**   **sedentary**

2. Words can be divided into *syllables*, i.e. single sounds. How many syllables has each of the following words?

   cough   **initiative**   **jeopardy**   **courier**   **indubitable**

3. Part of the correct pronunciation is putting *stress* on the right syllable. Re-read the note on page xii in the dictionary and then say which syllable in the following words is spoken with the most stress. Example:

   chaos is pronounced **kay**-oss, with the stress on the first of its two syllables.

   ionosphere   **medieval**   **inexorable**   **progress** *verb*

   progress *noun*

4. Repeat, aloud, all the words you have met on this page. Then try to put each one into a spoken sentence which shows how it can be used.

Phrases

The word **hang** generally means to support something from above. But what is meant by the phrases:

hang about**hang back****hang on****hang up?**

Phrases like these are called *idioms*. They have their own special meanings.

1 What is meant by the following idioms?
The headwords where you will find the idioms are in italics.

make **off** with the money
on the *move* again
get **your own back** on someone
come **by** a large sum of money
talking **behind** **a person's back**
back **out** of an agreement
play **down** a crisis
take a joke **in good** *part*
appear **in** *person*
be **on** *hand* in case of emergency

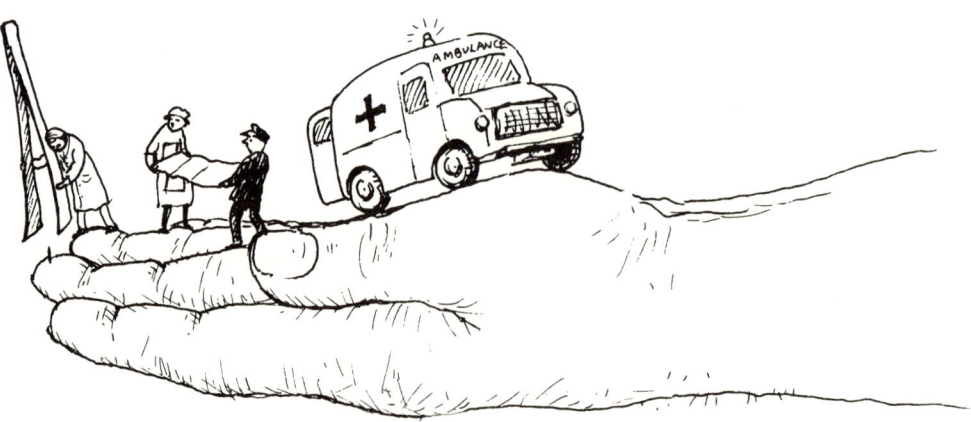

2 Many of the idioms given in the dictionary are marked by the word *(informal)*. What do you think this means? (You will find the answer at the front of the dictionary.)

3 Write down six idioms that you use frequently. Look to see if they are in the dictionary.

Usage

19

Be careful how you use some words.

Where a word is frequently used wrongly, or where there is a confusing similarity between two words, the dictionary warns you. For example:

curb *verb* restrain.
curb *noun* a restraint, *Put a curb on spending.* USAGE Do not confuse with *kerb*.

1 Look at the following pairs of sentences. In each case, say which sentence is correct.

a You must learn to curb your impatience.
b Don't step off the curb if there is traffic coming.

c There are two alternate styles to choose from.
d The strange craft was glowing in alternate colours.

e Being in Scotland at the time of the murder gave me an alibi.
f Saying that it was only an accident is no alibi.

g There was no mistaking her distinct way of dressing.
h This time the sound was quite distinct.

i There have been tales of strange phenomena at the house.
j Ghosts are one phenomena I can't bring myself to take seriously.

k The hotel accommodation was really luxuriant.
l Part of his disguise was a luxuriant black beard.

m My grandmother is a compulsive supporter of Liverpool F.C.
n It is compulsive to wear crash-helmets on site.

o It's no good trying to burn that: it's inflammable.
p Inflammable gases are a danger in coal mines.

2 Can you see a way of putting right each of the incorrect sentences above, without altering more than one word in each?

Connections

A game for two or more players

Start with any word chosen for you by your opponent. It has to be a word all the players know, for example:

build

The object is to guess a word which will be used in the dictionary definition of **build**, for example:

make

Look it up. If you are right, score a point and continue. If you are wrong, that is the end of your turn. As it happens, you are right:

build *verb* make something by putting parts together ...

So now try to guess a word which will appear in the definition for **make**. For example, you might say:

cause

Right again!

make *verb* ... 3 cause or compel.

Continue your turn, or 'break', until you get one wrong. This break, for instance, could continue:

cause > **happen** > **occur** > **be** > **exist** > **alive** ...

The winner is the player who scores the longest break.

Rules

You are not allowed to use the same word more than once in a break. You are not allowed to use the words:

is   are   the   a   an   and   or   to   from

You can disregard common endings of words, such as **-ed**, **-ing**, or **s**.

For example, look up **ivory**: if you had guessed *elephant* instead of *elephants*', it would count as being right.

Origo
Origins

21

English is a mixture of many languages. You can tell this by looking up the following words in the dictionary:

denim   finish   sugar   melody   billycan

bride   butler   potato   kiosk   mammoth

1 From which languages have the twelve words above come into Modern English?

2 What do the origins of the following words have in common?

dahlia   braille   welly   cardigan   sandwich   joule

3 The words in the next group have curious origins. Try to guess where they come from before looking them up.

deadline   juggernaut   lord   truncheon   laser   harass

thug   robot   tulip   tadpole   poll tax   dodo

4 These words have the same origin:

What is the origin? Copy the diagram and write the origin in the circle.

Draw similar diagrams showing the shared origins of these pairs or groups of words:

liberate   liberty

mortify   mortal

battle   battery   batter

vengeance   vindictive   vendetta

sign   signal   signature   signet

Appendices Append

Look up **January** and **Monday**. Whereabouts in the dictionary are these words to be found? (The *Contents* page at the front will help you.)

Now answer these questions:

1. What is a *prefix*? Underline the prefix in each of the following words:

    hexagon   omnivorous   distraction   universe   periscope

2. What is a *suffix*? Underline the suffix in each of these words:

    democracy   highest   clockwise   musician   telepathy

3. From which language have each of these expressions been borrowed? What do they mean in English?

    ad nauseam   doppelgänger   laissez-faire   hara-kiri

    sotto voce   eureka   faux pas   bona fide

4. From which language have the English names for the days of the week come down, and what are they all named after?

5. From which language have the English names for the months of the year come down?

6. What is the difference between an American pint and a British pint?

7. If the weather forecast tells you it is going to be eighty-six degrees Fahrenheit in the shade, what temperature can you expect on the Celsius scale?

Acrostic Definitions

Look up the word **acrostic**. What does it mean?

Here is an example of an acrostic in which each line is a definition, or part of a definition, of the word spelt by the initial letters:

Sun
Twinkling point of light in the night sky
A shape with several pointed arms
Really famous performer

The word is **STAR**.

1 If you rearrange these definitions, you can make an acrostic like the one in the example above. What is the word it spells?

Exert pressure
Verb used informally to mean 'throw'
Action of lifting something heavy
Hard push
Expend a lot of effort

2 Here there are *two* sets of definitions, or parts of definitions, mixed together. Can you sort them out into two separate *acrostic* definitions? What are the two words they spell?

Adjective meaning weak
Cul-de-sac, dead end
Even, well-matched
Faded
Nearly unconscious
Local
Indistinct
The opposite of clear
Of things that are near by
Stuffy

3 Try to make up one or two acrostic definitions of your own. Then mix them up and try them on someone else.

Part two Exploring language
Synonyms = Synonyms

The king had all his enemies thrown in **gaol**.
The king had all his enemies thrown in **prison**.

These two sentences mean the same, because **gaol** and **prison** are *synonyms*.

1. Find a synonym for each of the words in bold in the following sentences:

   You must **obtain** permission before you can camp here.
   What she said did not make a very **cogent** argument.
   Every **individual** vote has to be counted.
   I don't think you **appreciate** the **magnitude** of the problem.
   Some of the gang were **apprehended** at the airport.
   The members of the expedition planned their **itinerary meticulously**.
   This unexpected development **scuppered** our plans.
   The **odour** of stale tobacco smoke **permeated** the room.

2. Make up short sentences in which the following pairs of words mean the same. Follow the example for **gaol** and **prison** at the top of the page.

   abortive; unsuccessful   **variable; changeable**

   film; layer   **indirect; circuitous**   **flooded; inundated**

   tools; implements   **empty; void**   **tarnish; blemish**

3. Do you think there are any pairs of words that are always synonyms, whatever sentences they are used in? Experiment with the following words, and try to think up some examples of your own.

   die; perish   **slope; incline**   **freedom; liberty**

   incredible; unbelievable   **follow; pursue**

   What conclusion have you come to?

4. Why do you think there are so many English words with roughly the same meaning as the noun **smell**? For example:

   odour   aroma   stink   stench   whiff   pong   scent

   Are there certain occasions when you would use one word but not the others; and, if so, why?

What Kind? What Difference?

falcon *noun* a kind of hawk often used in the sport of hunting other birds or game. **falconry** *noun*

1 What kind of bird is a falcon?
  What makes a falcon different from other birds of the same kind?

  A useful way to define something is to say what it is like (its *kind*), and then what makes it special (its *difference*). For example:

WORD	KIND	DIFFERENCE
mayfly	insect	lives for a short time, in spring

2 What kinds and what differences does the dictionary give in its definitions of these words? Continue the table.

   hangar   mead   crocus   gondola   thirteen

3 The word for a kind is often called a *general term*. **Hawk** is a more general term than **falcon**; but **bird** is a more general term than **hawk**.

   With the help of the dictionary, put the following words into their order of generality, with the most general term first.

   fungus, mushroom, plant   snail, animal, gastropod

   communication, gossip, talk   offal, liver, sustenance

   mineral, matter, zinc, metal   biology, study, science, botany

4 Write your own short defintions for the following, saying what kind of thing each one is and what makes it different:

   skyscraper   submarine   constable   dictionary   moon

Opposites | Opposites

absent *adjective* not here; not present,
absent from school. **absence** *noun*

present and **absent** are *opposite* in meaning.

1. Write one word which is opposite in meaning to each of the following:

   far   fiction   concave   humble   stingy

2. Opposites are often formed by adding **un-** or **in-** to the beginning of a word. For example:

   exciting > unexciting

   Produce the opposites of the following adjectives in the same way:

   usual   frequent   expensive   prejudiced   sane

3. For each of the words you produced in the last exercise, find another word or short phrase which means the same. For example:

   unexciting = dull

4. What does each of these words mean, and what is its opposite?

   anticlimax   nonsense   irrelevant   immobile   posterior

5. What is the opposite of:
   i the **maximum** daytime temperature?
   ii a **deciduous** tree?
   iii someone who is an **extrovert**?
   iv **deducting** an amount?
   v **dissent**?
   vi a **regular** verb?
   vii a **descending** order?

Word Associations

27

Make a copy of this page; then make five chains of words which are associated in meaning. Use a different colour for each group.

Each chain ends in one of the boxes at the bottom of the page. In the box write one word which sums up what all the words in that chain are about.

One chain has been started and finished for you.

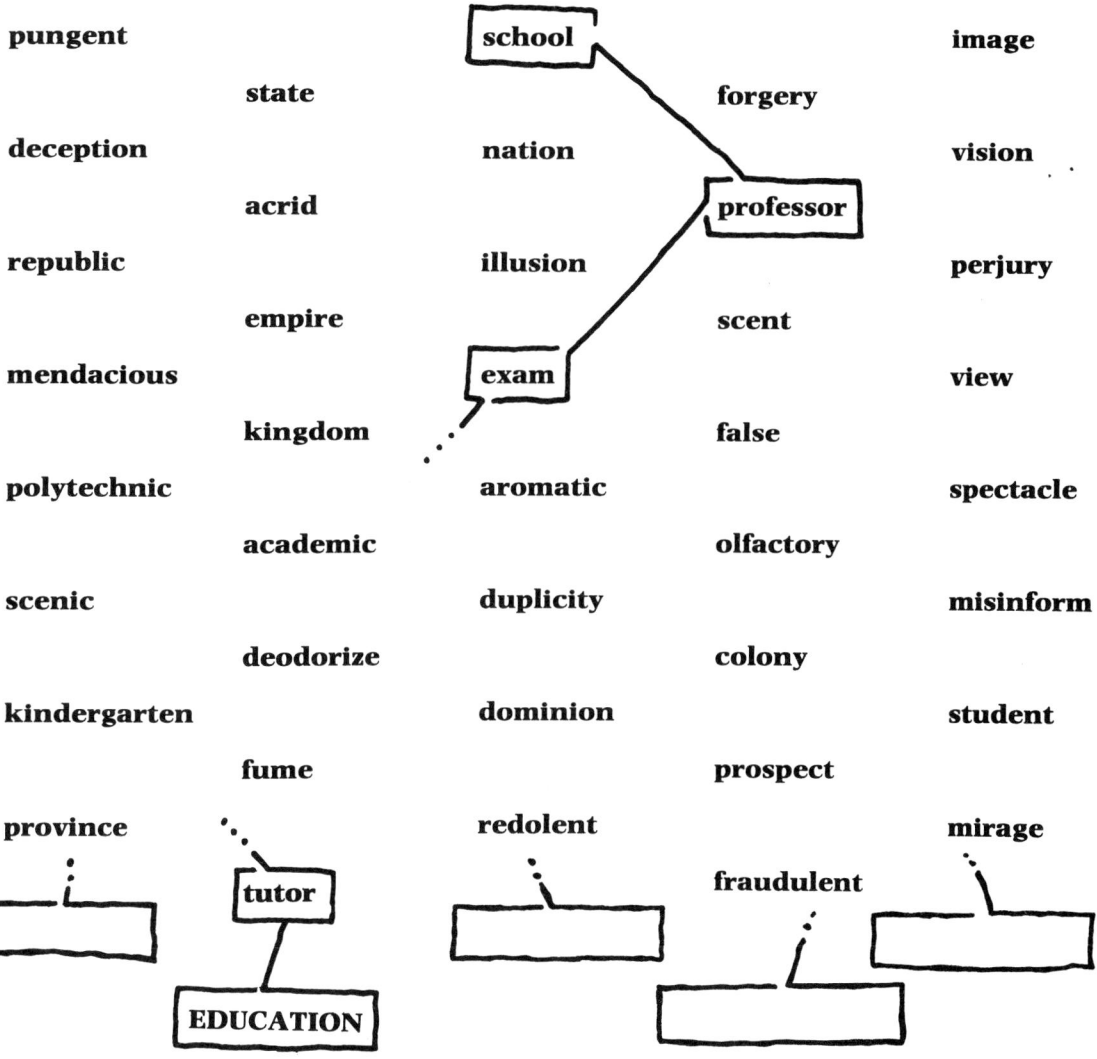

Male and Female

Many English words have a male and a female form. For example:

actor, actress   **husband, wife**

1 Put the following words into their correct male and female pairs:

dog   count   pen   maternal   drone   countess

vixen   feminine   cob   sire   paternal   masculine

bitch   niece   fox   queen   nephew   dam

2 What is the male equivalent of each of these words?

stewardess   heroine   manageress   sisterly   horsewoman

fiancée   femininity   Dame   bride

3 Which pairs of words, one male and one female, is covered by each of these nouns? For example, **child** covers **boy** and **girl**.

fowl   sibling   monarch   parent   foal

Discussion

Many English words end or begin with man. For instance:

spokesman   chairman   henchman   foreman

manpower   manslaughter   mankind

In which of these words should **woman** or **person** sometimes, or always, be used instead?

Think of some other, similar examples.

An **actress**, or a **waitress** has to be female, but a **doctor**, a **mechanic** or a **surveyor** can be male or female. Put together a list of occupations: how many have separate male and female titles?

You could have a class or group debate on the complaint that:

The English Language is sexist and needs to be changed!

Compound Words

1. Look up **compound**[1] in the dictionary and write down what you think a compound word is.

2. The opposite of **compound** is **simple**. Which of the following are simple words and which are compound words?

   water   fall   waterfall   breakwater   break

3. Find five more compound words and write them down together with the simple words that form them. For example:

   lifetime = life + time

4. Some compound words are *hyphenated*, i.e. the simple words that form them are joined by a dash called a *hyphen*.

   Write down the compound words which are formed from the following pairs of words, showing which ones require a hyphen and which ones do not.

life + jacket	**light + house**	**main + land**
sand + paper	**set + up**	**nanny + goat**
frame + work	**lift + off**	**pick + pocket**

5. **banknote**
       notepaper
           paperback
               background
                   ground ...

   Can you make this *word-stair* longer?

   Make up some *word-stairs* of your own, using compound words.

6. The words **out** and **look** can be used to form *two* compound words,

   outlook   look-out

   Can you think of any other pairs or words which do this? (There is one example in question four.)

Prefixes

A *prefix* is an attachment to the beginning of a word. It has a meaning, but it is not a complete word. For example:

inter- *prefix* between; among. [from Latin]

1. Look up **inter-** in the dictionary and make a rough count of the number of words that begin with this prefix.

2. If you remove the prefix **inter-** from the beginning of the word **international**, you are left with another, shorter word. What is it?

   Do the same with the following words:

   interchange   interplanetary   interview   interdependent

3. Say what each of the following prefixes means and give two examples of its use in forming words:

   multi-   mono-   equi-   semi-   poly-

   Can you see what these five prefixes have in common?

4. Look up the entry for **sub-** *prefix*.

   i. What are the two meanings of **sub-**?
   ii. In how many different ways can this prefix be spelt? Give an example of each one.

5. Copy and finish filling in the grid below

	pre-	**re-**	**ex-**	**anti-**
t	pretend	retire		
a	prearrange			anti-**a**ircraft
f				
s				
v				

   Make up a similar grid with other letters and prefixes. You could invent a game using the grid, and play it within your group.

Suffixes

Look at the list of *suffixes* on pages 456-458 in the dictionary. What is the difference between a *prefix* and a *suffix*?

1. The suffix **-less** means 'without'. The example given in the dictionary is **colourless**, i.e. without colour.

   Make up a short sentence to show what each of these words means:

   hopeless   merciless   countless   ageless   useless   mindless

2. The opposite of **colourless** is **colourful**. How many other words from question one have opposites ending with the suffix **-ful**?

   Do any of the following have opposites ending with **-less**?

   awful   resentful   playful   thoughtful   handful   harmful

3. Often the spelling of a word has to be altered before a certain suffix can be added. For example:

   mercy + -less > merciless

   Copy out and complete the following:

   lazy + -est > ...

   explode + -ive > ...

   intend + -ion > ...

   pure + -ification > ...

   telephone + -ist > ...

4. The word *affix* can be used to mean any addition to a word, whether it is a prefix or a suffix. What shorter words are you left with if you strip the affixes from the following?

   plantation   premeditation   unofficially

   immortalize   consolidate   postscript

Roots Roots Roots Roots Roots Roots

Many English words can be seen to grow from the same *root*. The root **STRUCT**, for example, can be used in the formation of **construct, construction, structure** and others.

1. How many words can you build from this 'kit'?

   im-   de-   com-   sup-   ex-

   PRESS

   -ive   -ure   -ion

2. Copy the table below; then form ten words and link them to their meanings by drawing connecting lines. One is done for you.

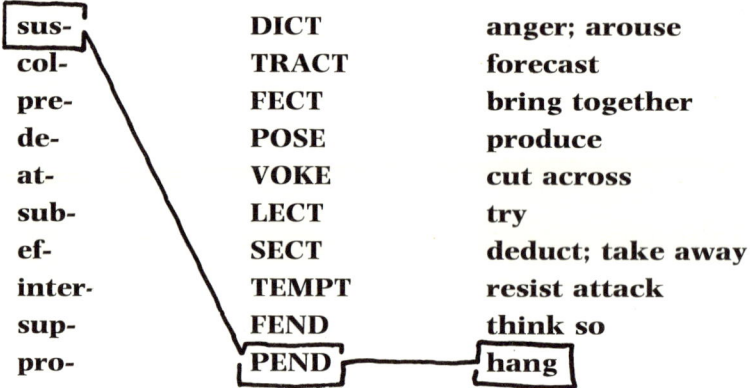

sus-	DICT	anger; arouse
col-	TRACT	forecast
pre-	FECT	bring together
de-	POSE	produce
at-	VOKE	cut across
sub-	LECT	try
ef-	SECT	deduct; take away
inter-	TEMPT	resist attack
sup-	FEND	think so
pro-	PEND	hang

3. One root completes all the words in each row. Select the right ones from the list at the end.

   cor ... ion   dis ... ive   ... ure   inter ...

   im ...   ex ...   ... er   sup ... er   ... able   re ... er

   pre ... ence   con ... ence   inter ... ence

   FER   PENT   SENT   RUPT   PORT   RECT

In many words the spelling and pronunciation of the root are affected by the ending that follows it. For example:

describe > descriptive   delude > delusion

1 What nouns ending in **-ion** are formed from the following verbs?

produce   proceed   extend   expel   invade   receive   admit

2 What adjectives ending **-ive** are formed from these verbs?

exclude   destroy   explode   defend   exceed   deceive

3 **i** Look up the word tractor. What nearby word has the same origin?

ii Tractor is formed from the root **TRACT** which means pull or drag. Which word, from the root **TRACT**, fits each one of the spaces below?

When a cat pulls *back* its claws, it ... them.
When a magnet draws something *towards* it, it ... it.
When a dentist *pulls* a tooth out, she ... it.

iii Write a phrase or short sentence containing each of these words:

protracted   contract   traction   detracts   intractable

4 **i** Look up **torsion**. What does it mean?

ii What word with the same root means each of the following?

A person who twists money out of someone by force or threats.
A person who twists his or her body into unusual shapes.
A person who deliberately causes pain or suffering to someone.

Word Stems

The *stem* is the main part of a word. By adding different endings to it you can form different words which are connected in meaning. For example:

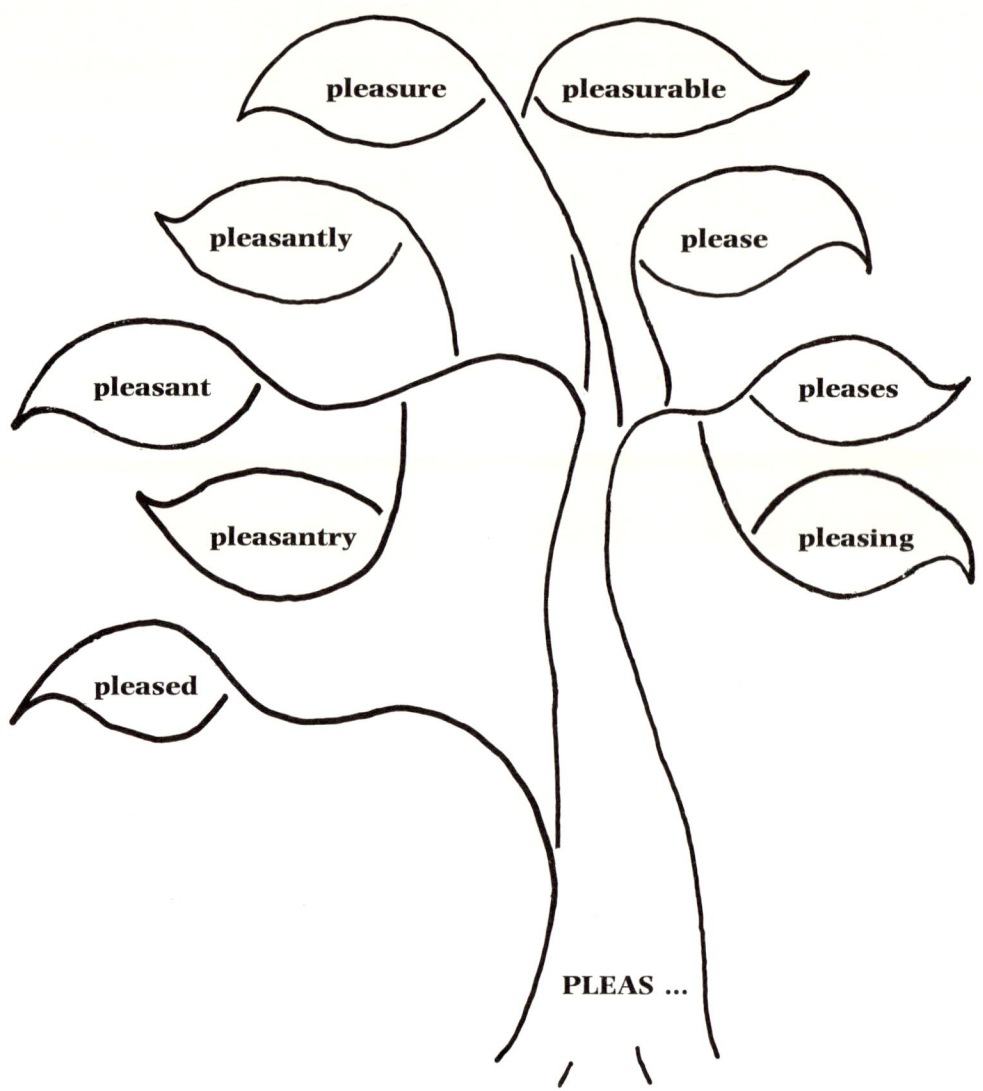

1. Construct a similar tree diagram with the stem **MANAG ...** ; and another with a word stem of your own choice.

Inflect
Inflexions

Look at the entry for **inflect**, and **read** and discuss the note on *Inflexions* and *Plurals* in The Oxford School Dictionary.

1 Write down the correct inflexions of the verb **see** in the following examples. Each one should be different.

> I don't want to ... you here again.
> She suddenly ... something out of the corner of her eye.
> We haven't ... him around here recently.
> I'll be ... you.
> I honestly don't know what she ... in him.

2 The most inflected verb in English is **be**. How many different forms does the dictionary give, and what are they?

3 Look up the words **them** and **us** in the dictionary. When are they used instead of the forms **they** and **we**? Give examples.

4 **We** and **they** belong to the class *pronoun*. Some other pronouns also have inflexions:

I, me   she, her   he, him

Discuss the way the pronouns have been used in these sentences. Are any of them not Standard English; and, if not, why not?

> Me and him are good mates.
> Him and her ought to stop arguing all the time.
> Jasbir and I want to swap jobs.
> The money belongs to Stephen and I.
> Colin and me won the doubles championship.

5 Write down the plural forms of

this woman   that man

Research

As European languages go, English has very few inflexions. In your next foreign language lesson, find out how many forms there are for the verb meaning 'see' in French or Spanish or German.

The Origins of English

England's position on the edge of Europe, and its stormy history, have meant that the English language has undergone many changes.

Before discussing and answering the questions below, read pages vi and vii in the section entitled *The English Language*, at the front of the dictionary. Also look at the map and time-chart.

1 What language would have been spoken in Britain, do you think, if there had been no invasions or conquests in the last two thousand years?

2 Who were the three main invaders to land in Britain between the fifth and eleventh centuries? Which languages did they bring with them?

3 What is the origin of the word **English**?

4 Make four short lists of English words or names which have:

   i Celtic origins
   ii Anglo-Saxon origins
   iii Norse origins
   iv Norman French origins

Discussion

It is sometimes claimed that a person speaking Welsh and a person speaking Breton (the language of Brittany in north-west France) can understand each other. If this is true, why do you think it is so?

Research

Can you name a ruler in Britain who was:

   i Celtic?
   ii Anglo-Saxon?
   iii Danish?
   iv French?

Develop
How Words Develop

1. The Latin word *manus* meant 'hand'. From it originate several English words to do with hands, or doing or making things by hand. For example:

   manufacture

   Can you find any other words which share the same origin? Write them down, with their meanings alongside.

2. Look up:

   manufacture   benefactor   artefact   fact   factory   facsimile

   What is the connection between all these words, and what does each one mean?

3. What are the following?

   polygon   hexagon   pentagon   octagon

   From which language do they all originate?

4. Look up:

   algebra   geometry   arithmetic

   Which is the odd one out, and why?

5. Guess the origins of these words and then look them up:

   alligator   bonfire   budget   derrick   meteor

   malaria   mayday   mousse   nausea   racket

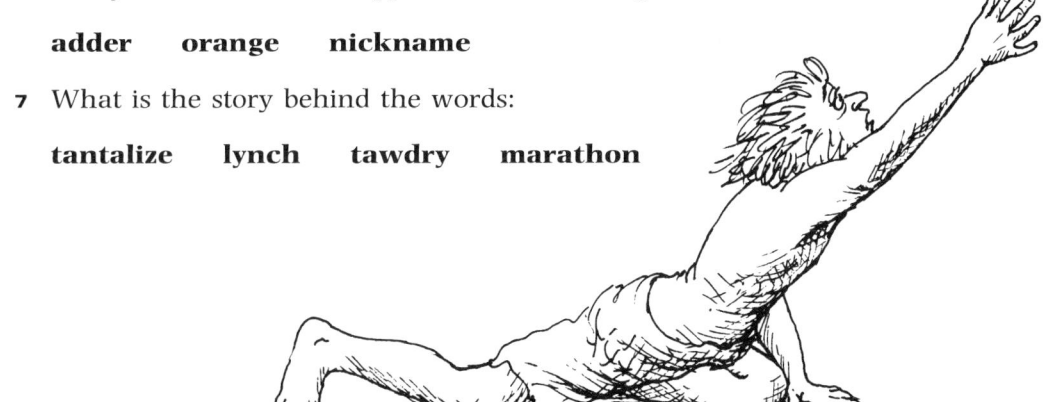

6. Can you see what has happened in the development of these words?

   adder   orange   nickname

7. What is the story behind the words:

   tantalize   lynch   tawdry   marathon

Language Groups

The languages of the world can be put into groups that have some similarities and shared history.

English belongs to the *Germanic* group of languages. Others in this group are German, Dutch, Flemish, and the Scandinavian languages, such as Danish.

Another closely related group of languages consists of those that developed from Latin. They are called *Romance* languages, and include French, Italian, Portuguese, and Spanish.

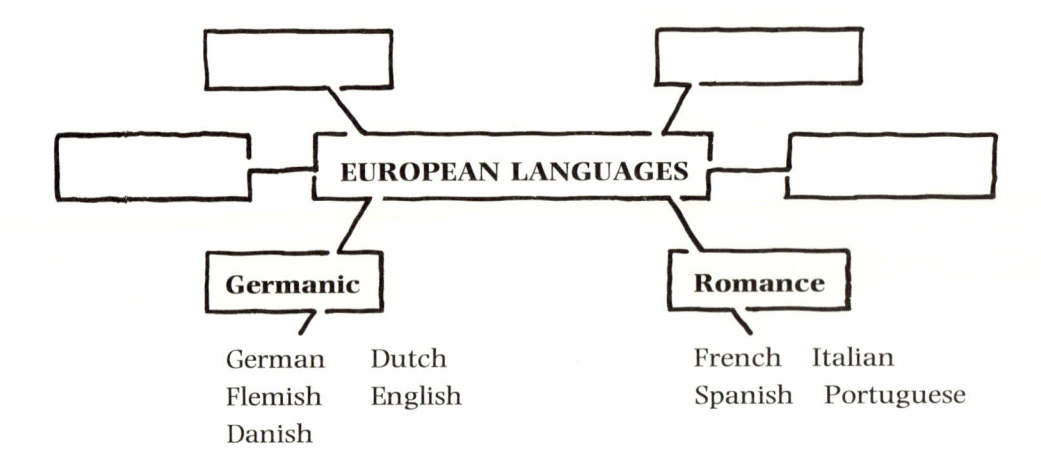

EUROPEAN LANGUAGES

Germanic

German   Dutch
Flemish English
Danish

Romance

French   Italian
Spanish Portuguese

1. Trace or copy the outline map of western Europe on the opposite page. With the help of an atlas indicate the countries where the following languages are spoken. Colour-code them: one colour for Germanic languages and another for Romance.

   Dutch   English   Flemish   French
   German Italian   Portuguese   Spanish   Danish

2. Why do you think that French, Italian, and Spanish, etc. are called Romance languages?

3. Compare your map with the map and time-chart on page vii in the dictionary. Why do you think English is called a Germanic language and not a Romance language?

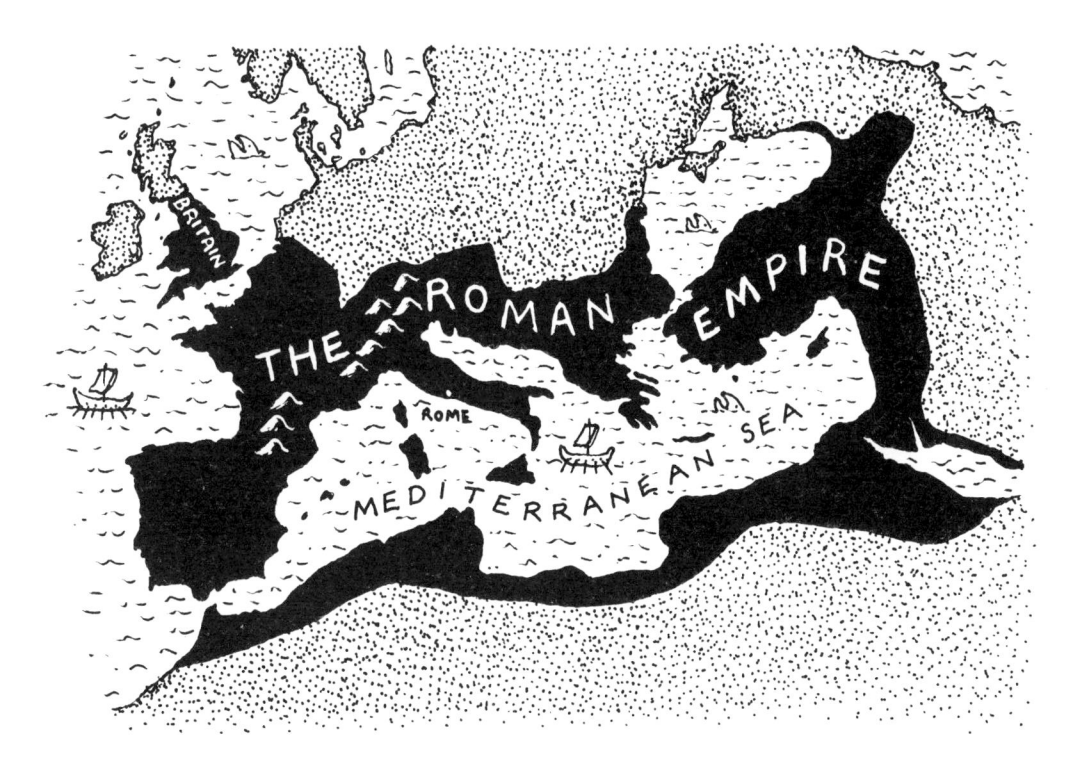

Discussion and Research

Why do you think the diagram on page 38 has some empty boxes? What belongs in them?

Find out some more about European language groups. Then copy or redesign the diagram so that you can add your new information to it.

Old English

Old English is the language that was spoken by the Angles and Saxons who invaded Britain and settled there from around AD 450.

Discussion

On the opposite page is a short piece of Old English, and below it is an approximate translation into Modern English.

How many words and phrases can you recognize in the passage as being similar to the English of today?

Apart from the words themselves, do you notice any other major differences between Old English and Modern English?

Why do you think the translation is only approximate?

1 Find out from the dictionary how these words were spelt in Old English

   father   mother   brother   husband   bride

2 i What were the original meanings of the words **lord** and **lady** and how have these words changed in meaning since Anglo-Saxon times?

   ii The words **well**[1] and **well**[2] are *homographs* (see page 7). So are **barrow**[1] and **barrow**[2]. Were the pairs of Old English words that they came from also homographs, or were they spelt differently?

   iii The Modern English word **barn** comes from two Old English words compressed into one. What were the two words and what did they mean?

Research

   serpent   snake

What are the origins of these two words, and how do they help to explain why English often has two or more names for the same thing?

With the help of a larger dictionary, or other reference books, see if you can find some more examples of duplicated words, like serpent and snake.

Ond þy ylcan gere worhte se foresprecana here geweorc be Lygan, xx mila bufan Lundenbyrig. Þa þæs on sumera foron micel dæl þara burgwara, ond eac swa oþres folces, þæt hie gedydon æt þara Deniscana geweorce, ond þær wurdon gefliemde, ond sume feower cyninges þegnas ofslægene. Þa þæs on hærfeste þa wicode se cyng on neaweste þære byrig, þa hwile þe hie hira corn gerypon, þæt þa Deniscan him ne mehton þæs ripes forwiernan. Þa sume dæge rad se cyng up bi þære eæ, ond gehawade hwær mon mehte þa ea forwyrcan, þæt hie ne mehton þa scipu ut brengan. Ond hie ða swa dydon: worhton ða tu geweorc on twa healfe þære eas.

Part of the account of King Alfred's wars with the Danes from The Anglo-Saxon Chronicle, AD 896.

(The symbols ð and þ are both pronounced like **th**; the symbol æ is usually pronounced like the **a** in **sat**; and **sc** is pronounced like the **sh** in **she**.)

And in the same year the aforementioned army built a fort by the Lea, twenty miles above London. Then later in the summer a large part of the population, and other forces as well, came to the Danish fort, and were put to flight and some four of the king's thanes (noblemen) were killed. Then the next autumn the king camped in the neighbourhood of the fort while they reaped their corn so that the Danes could not prevent the harvest. Then one day the king rode up by the river and looked to see where the river might be blocked so that they could not bring out the ships. And they did so: built two forts on the two sides of the river.

Middle English

Re-read the section on Middle English in the dictionary.

1 For a long time after the Norman Conquest in 1066, there were two languages spoken in England. What were they and who were they spoken by?

2 List six new words which came into use in England after the Norman Conquest.

Look at the piece of poetry on the opposite page. It was written towards the end of the fourteenth century. We call the stage the language had reached by then, Middle English.

Discussion

What main differences can you detect between the Old English passage on page 41 and this piece of Middle English?

What proportion of the words and phrases in the extract are easily recognizable?

What differences do you notice between this passage and Modern English?

The Knight's Tale

Whilom, as olde stories tellen us,
Ther was a duc that highte Theseus;
Of Atthenes he was lord and governour,
And in his tyme swich a conquerour,
That gretter was ther noon under the sonne.
Ful many a rich contree hadde he wonne;
What with his wysdom and his chivalrie,
He conquered al the regne of Femenye,
That whilom was ycleped Scithia,
And weddede the queene Ypolita,
And broughte hire hoom with hym in his contree
With muchel glorie and greet solempnytee,
And eek hir yonge suster Emylye.
And thus with victorie and with melodye
Lete I this noble duc to Atthenes ryde,
And al his hoost in armes hym besyde.

From The Canterbury Tales, by Geoffrey Chaucer

Latin

Latin was the language of the Romans, who, for centuries, occupied large parts of Europe, including Britain.

1. With the help of the notes on Middle English in the dictionary, answer the following questions.

    i Describe three different ways in which Latin words may have found their way into the English language.

    ii English has many more Latin words in it now than it had in the ninth century. Why do you think this is?

    iii How did the words, **mint**, **pound**, **sack** and **street** find their way into English?

2. Some Latin words have become English words without any change to the spelling, although their meanings and pronunciation may have altered. Look up the following and give their English and Latin meanings.

    interim   posterior   minimum   omnibus   extra

3. Some Latin nouns have even kept their original plural forms. What are the plurals of these words, and what do they mean? (Write the answers and say the words aloud to a partner.)

    formula   curriculum   opus   genus   fungus

4. **plus** and **minus** are words we use every day in mathematics. What did they mean in Latin?

5. What did the following words mean in Latin and what do they mean now?

    ego   exit   ludo   circus   campus   video

6. The Romans gave us the word **mile**. How was a mile originally measured?

Many of the prefixes that begin English words have been borrowed from Latin.

1. i The Latin word for *round* was 'circum'. How many words can you find in the dictionary which have **circum-** as a prefix?

   ii What English words could mean the following?

   sail completely *round* something: an island or the world, for instance;
   draw a line *round* something;
   avoid something, possibly by going *round* it;
   the distance a*round* the outside of something;
   the facts sur*round*ing some event or happening.

2. Many groups of English words have Latin roots. The root **-rect-**, for example, comes from the Latin word 'rectus', meaning straight or right.

   Can you think of six more English words which share this origin?

3. **progress   aggression   congress   regression**

   What does each of these words mean?
   What has each of the words got to do with 'going'?
   Of the four words, pick two that are *opposite* in meaning.

Greek

Look at the paragraph on Greek in the dictionary.

1. When was the period of history known as the *Renaissance*, and why did so many Greek words come into the English language at that time?

2. Explain the meaning of the word **atmosphere**. How has it got its meaning from Greek words?

3. **comedy   tragedy   theatre**

   What do these three words mean, and what were their original Greek meanings?

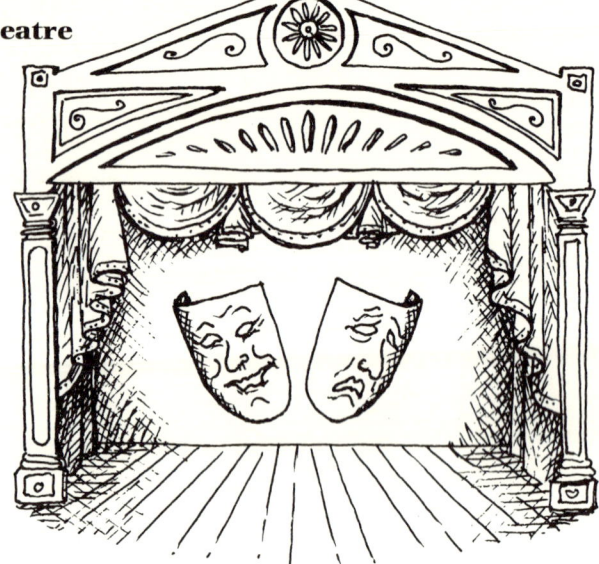

4. Find, from the Appendix in the dictionary, what the suffix **-graphy** means, and what it meant in Greek.

   Give some examples of words which have this ending.

5. List five words which end in **-logy**. What did this suffix mean in Greek?

6. How many words can you find that begin with the letters **phys-**? What did *physis* and *physikos* mean in Greek?

7. What do the following words have in common, and which Greek word or words does each one originate from?

   autopsy   anaesthetic   physiotherapy   antibiotic   pathology

   Can you add three words which could belong to the list and which also have Greek origins? Think of words to do with medicine.

Science and Technology

lift-off *noun* the vertical take-off of a rocket or spacecraft.

1. The American space programme during the last thirty years has given the language many new words and expressions - or new meanings for existing words. What do the following mean?

   module   capsule   astronaut   shuttle

2. What new science do these expressions belong to, and what do they mean?

   software   hardware   byte   VDU   floppy disk

3. The following new sports have resulted from modern technology:

   windsurfing   hang-gliding   skateboarding

   Write a dictionary-style entry of your own for each of these words; then compare it with the one in *The Oxford School Dictionary*.

4. What are:

   acid rain   plutonium   ozone layer   asbestos   radioactivity?

5. What are:

   nylon   polymers   polystyrene   vinyl   melamine?

6. What do the following have in common?

   watts   amps   joules   hertz   Celsius

7. What are the origins of the words:

   science   technology   physics   chemistry   atomic   zoology?

Word Travels

A game for two or more players

The English language has travelled all over the world. On its travels it has absorbed many words from other countries.

The object of this game is to circumnavigate the globe, with the help of words. You will need two counters.

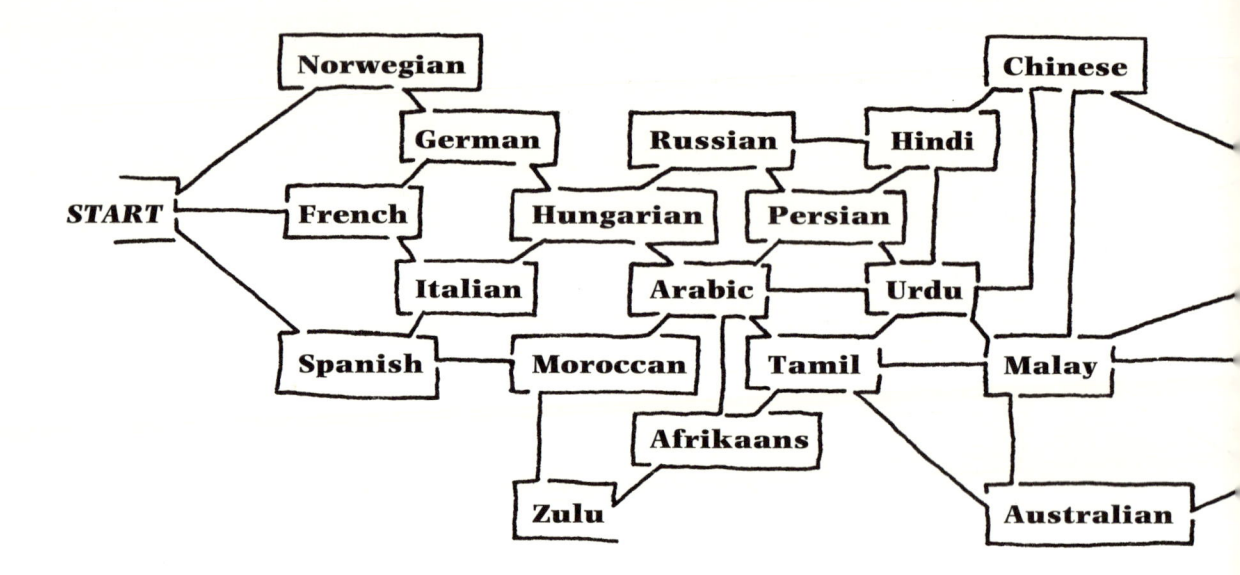

```
                Norwegian                              Chinese
                      German        Russian      Hindi
START         French        Hungarian    Persian
                    Italian         Arabic        Urdu
           Spanish       Moroccan        Tamil        Malay
                              Afrikaans
                         Zulu                    Australian
```

amok   battalion   cherish   magazine   pyjamas
barracks   orange   tomahawk   chocolate   skiing
shampoo   poppadam   typhoon   tangerine

How to play

In each turn you can look up one word from the list at the bottom of the page. If it comes from the language or nationality marked in a square directly connected to the one you are on, show the entry to everyone and move to the new square. If not, keep it to yourself and remember it for later in the game. *Bon voyage!*

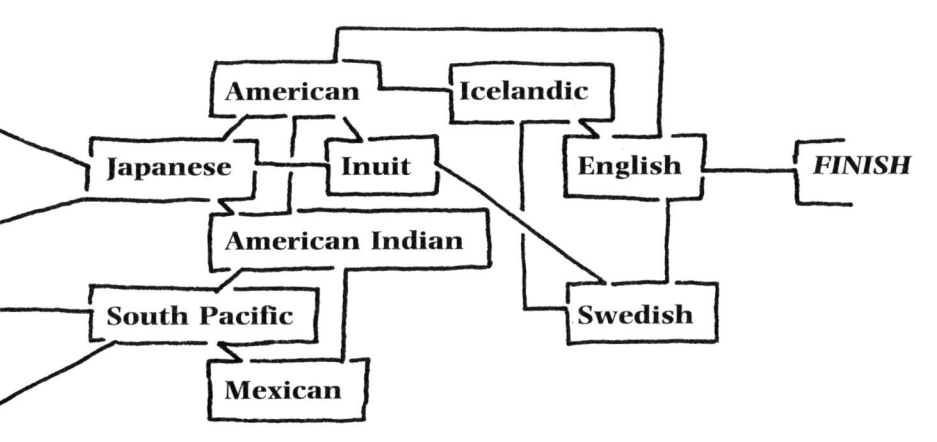

```
            American ─── Icelandic
  Japanese ─┤  Inuit  ├──  English ── FINISH
            American Indian
  South Pacific        Swedish
            Mexican
```

berserk   rucksack   billabong   glasnost   biro
bikini   rooster   impala   kayak   origami   apartheid
tungsten   cheap

Rules

You may only move along the connecting lines - one square per turn. You may not move to a square which has an opponent's counter on it. You may not write anything down during the game.

Those and These
Nouns and Pronouns

Pronouns are substitute words. They can be used in place of nouns, and are particularly useful to avoid repetition.

The van badly needed a service. *It* hadn't had *one* in years.

1. How would you have to write the second sentence if there were no such words as pronouns?

2. With the help of the entry for **pronoun**, write out a sample set of pronouns, adding, if you can, a few more examples to those given in the dictionary.

   pronoun: { ... }

3. Which of the pronouns in your set are plural words?

   Which of the pronouns in your set are called *personal* pronouns? Why do you think they are called this?

   Which of the pronouns in your set are used to ask questions?

   Which of the pronouns in your set are used to point to things or people?

   Which of the pronouns in your set are used to express belonging?

   Which of the pronouns in your set are old-fashioned words, except in some dialects?

4. Every English noun is either a *he*, a *she*, an *it*, or a *they*.

   What **they**, beginning with **n**, is:

   (first clue)   an ingredient of soups etc?
   (second clue)   cut into narrow strips?
   (third clue)   made of pasta?

   If you still haven't got it, it begins **noo** ...

   There are some more questions like these on the opposite page. Before you start, place a sheet of paper over them so that you can uncover the clues one at a time. Keep your own score: three if you get it right after the first clue, two after the second and one after the third.

He, She, It, or They?
A quiz

1 What *it* beginning with **p** is

   (first clue)   a mixture of lime, sand, and water?
   (second clue)   used for covering walls and ceilings?
   (third clue)   used for setting broken bones?

2 What *she* beginning with **s** is

   (first clue)   a nun?
   (second clue)   a daughter of the same parents as someone else?
   (third clue)   a hospital nurse in charge of others?

3 What *they* beginning with **m**

   (first clue)   are extinct?
   (second clue)   had curved tusks?
   (third clue)   looked like large, hairy elephants?

4 What *it* beginning with **s** is

   (first clue)   a small piece of cork or plastic with a crown of feathers?
   (second clue)   hit with a racket?
   (third clue)   used in a game of badminton?

5 What *it* beginning with **b** is

   (first clue)   bought cheaply?
   (second clue)   a deal?
   (third clue)   an agreement about buying or selling something?

6 What *it* beginning with **s** is

   (first clue)   a country that is under the influence of another more powerful country?
   (second clue)   a moon?
   (third clue)   an object that moves in orbit around a planet?

7 What *it* beginning with **i** is

   (first clue)   an effect produced on the mind?
   (second clue)   a vague idea?
   (third clue)   an imitation of a person's voice or mannerisms?

Top score possible: 21

Adjectives

Look up the meaning of the word **adjective** in the dictionary, and look at the sample adjectives below:

fierce   fine   fragile   formidable   frantic

1 i Which of the sample adjectives could meaningfully fit each of these noun phrases?

a ... line   ... signals
a ... problem   ... opposition
a ... agreement

Some will fit more than one phrase.

ii Can you find five different adjectives all beginning with the same letter, that would fit the same five noun phrases?

2 Many English adjectives have three forms. They are called the **positive**, **comparative** and **superlative**. Look up these words, then copy and complete the table below:

POSITIVE	COMPARATIVE	SUPERLATIVE
big	bigger	biggest
small		
happy		
wide		
heavy		
few		
shy		
good		
bad		
cruel		
stocky		
sad		
much		
many		

Check that you have correctly spelt the comparative and superlative forms, by looking them up.

If no comparative or superlative forms are given in the dictionary, what is the rule for spelling them?

1 Under which headword do each of the following adjectives appear in the dictionary, and which word class does the headword belong to?

mythological   national   progressive   proportional   crinkly

2 i What adjectives are given as derivatives of these headwords:

discern   hypnotize   mutiny   photography   spectre

ii Make up five short sentences to include the five adjectives you have just collected.

3 As well as making up noun phrases, adjectives can also be used as *complements*.

Look up **complement**, especially definition 2. Which of the two examples of complements that the dictionary gives, is an adjective:

brave or **king of England**?

Complete these sentences with adjectives:

Some breeds of dogs are ... .   The sky looked ... .

The journey seemed ... .   The food tasted ... .

Check in the dictionary that the complement you have chosen is an adjective.

4 Replace the adjectives in bold with another word or phrase which means the same:

In many houses the kitchen and bathroom are **communal**.
My sister was **overwrought**.
The painting doesn't look **authentic** to me.
It is dangerous for a referee to appear too **lax**.
This problem is **perennial**.

Complements
A game for any number of players

Make up a list of nouns or phrases, each followed by the words 'is', 'was', 'are', or 'were'. You can start with the following or make up your own:

School is ...   Washing up is ...   Many people were ...

The oceans are ...   London is ...   The sky was ...

Choose a letter of the alphabet. Ask someone to say 'Go', and write down *a single word*, beginning with that letter, to complement each of the phrases. (You cannot use the same word twice.)

SCHOOL IS BAFFLING

MANY PEOPLE ARE BOWING

LONDON IS BIG

The first to finish says 'Stop,' and earns an extra two points on his or her score. Players take it in turns to read out their completed sentences; if two or more players have chosen the same word, they must cross it out. One point is then scored for every complement that no one else has thought of.

You can use the dictionary. The resulting sentences must make sense.

Adverbs

Adverbs are words which tell us *how*, *when* or *where* something happens.

adverb: {**quickly**, **carelessly**, **yesterday**, **late**, **here**, **there**, ...}

Many English adverbs are formed from adjectives by attaching the suffix **-ly**. Usually you just add **-ly** without change, but there are some exceptions.

reliable *adjective* able to be relied on; trustworthy. **reliably** *adverb*, **reliability** *noun*

1 Write down the adverbs that are formed from these adjectives:

   thoughtful   happy   frantic   full   shy   gay   late   preferable

2 A **punctual** person is likely to arrive **punctually**. What sort of person is likely to do the following?

   mix **sociably** with other people
   watch **morosely** whilst other people enjoy themselves
   tidy everything away **fastidiously**
   rush into things **impetuously**
   sneer **contemptuously** at others
   act **magnanimously**

3 Look at the entry for the suffix **-ly** in the Appendix. Which other class of words, besides adverbs, often ends with these letters?

   To which word class does each of the following belong?

   gently   friendly   prickly   purposely   cuddly

Actions

Verbs are sometimes described as action words, but many action words can also be used as nouns.

cough (*say* kof) *verb* send out air from the lungs with a sudden sharp sound.
cough *noun* 1 the act or sound of coughing. 2 an illness that makes you cough.

1 Write two short sentences, one using **cough** as a verb, the other using **cough** as a noun.

2 Which of the following verbs can also be used as nouns?

sneeze gain sleep betray forget go treat stay

Which of the following nouns can also be used as verbs?

deposit shadow paddle relay snow mill mirror food

Answer these questions by placing all sixteen words on a Venn diagram.

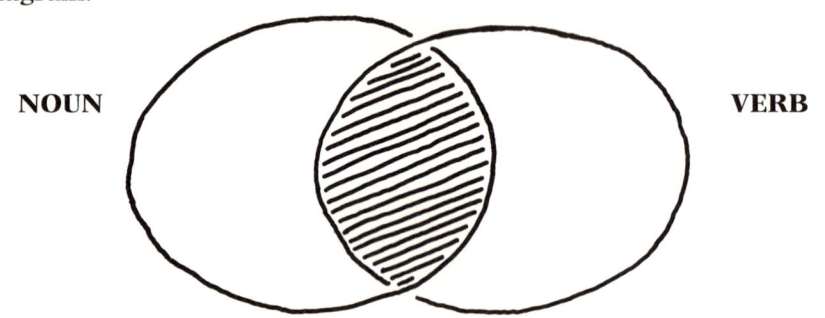

NOUN   **VERB**

Do some of the words belong in the *intersection* (the shaded part); and if so, why?

3 Many nouns that denote actions are formed from verbs by adding a suffix or changing the spelling.

arrive *verb* > **arrival** *noun*

What nouns are formed from the following verbs?

succeed descend deride refuse impede speak expire denounce

Use each of the nouns you have collected in a phrase or short sentence.

Feelings

despair *noun* a feeling of hopelessness.
despair *verb* feel despair. [from *de-*, + Latin *sperare* = to hope]

1 The following nouns all denote feelings or emotions. They are listed in a certain order, sometimes called a *spectrum*. Can you see what the order is?

elation   hope   indifference   pessimism   despair

Do you think that any of the following extra words belong to the same spectrum, and if so where do they fit in?

jubilation   ecstasy   misery   despondency   guilt

2 Adjectives can be used to describe how someone feels. For example,

I felt **desperate**.

Use adjectives to say how you would be feeling if you were experiencing each of the other nine emotions found in question 1.

Group work: Miming

Write each of the words in the box below on a small piece of paper and fold it. Give one to each person. (There may be some left over for a second round.)

If you don't know its meaning, look up your word in the dictionary; then mime it for the others, who must try to identify which word is yours. They too may consult the dictionary if they want to.

Points: Plus-one for a correct identification. Minus-one for an incorrect guess.

irascible	**desolate**	**snubbed**	**impassive**	**dejected**
circumspect	**harassed**	**impetuous**	**reticent**	**exhilarated**

When these words have run out, try finding some more of your own. As well as the dictionary, a *thesaurus* could help you find new words for this activity.

True or False?
A quiz

Decide, or guess, whether each of these statements is true or false. Then use the dictionary to find out if you were right.

1 The word **jamb**, meaning a side post of a doorway or window frame, comes from the French word for a leg.

2 **laconic** and **terse** are synonyms.

3 An **interval** was originally the space between ramparts on a fortress.

4 **liberal** and **library** have the same root and origin.

5 The five-line verses called **limericks** were named after a German poet.

6 **lavish**, meaning generous, used to mean a downpour of rain.

7 **liquid** and **liquorice** come from the same Latin root.

8 **maelstrom** means whirlpool.

9 **molars**, the big teeth at the back of the jaw, are named after millstones.

10 **parasite** once meant 'guest at a meal'.

11 A **steeplechase** is so called because the race originally had a church steeple in view as a goal.

12 A **tactician** is someone who shows a lot of tact.

13 **Koala** bears are found only in Africa.

14 **krill** is the name of a tiny fish.

15 The word **trek**, meaning travel a long way on foot, comes from Alaska in the USA.

What's the Connection?
A quiz

Can you discover, from the dictionary, some connection between the following pairs of words or things?

1 a rainbow and an iris

2 a washing line and a linen sheet

3 an officer in command of a regiment and the inside part of a nut

4 the words island and insulation

5 insect larvae and ghosts

6 applause and an explosion

7 a tail and a queue

8 state of Utopia and nowhere

9 tallness and swiftness

10 an interlude and a game

11 a planet and a wanderer

12 silage and missiles

13 chess and a former ruler of Iran

14 the words business and pigeon

15 a Tory and an outlaw

New Words

Some words are very old: they go so far back that no one can be sure of the exact origins. But some words have come into our language quite recently.

1. Look up the word **chauvinism**. What did it mean originally, and what does it mean now? What is the approximate age of the word?

    two hundred years   five hundred years   a thousand years

2. **motel**, **moped** and **smog** are new English words made by combining two existing words. What are the words that have been combined in each case?

    Can you think of some other words that have been formed in this way?

3. The following words name or describe new objects:

    slot-machine   hamburger   juke-box   keyboard   T-shirt

    high-rise   turnstile   torpedo   disco   barbecue

    Try to find out, or guess, how each of these words originated.

4. Many new words have been constructed out of old parts. What do the following words mean and what do their parts mean?

    television   parachute   aqualung   locomotive   transistor

    photograph   minibus   supermarket   contraflow   microchip

5. Some words are shortenings of older or longer words. What are the full versions of these?

    pram   bus   taxi   bike   fridge   zoo

New words and expressions are being invented all the time to describe new events or activities. Some of these are old words that have been given new life, for example, **poll tax**.

Some are foreign words that have become part of everyday life, for example, **kebab**.

Some are words that have been made from others, for example, **trainers** (from training shoes).

Some are spelt from the initials of a phrase, for example **radar**.

Discussion and group work

Can you think of any other new words, especially words that you or your friends use? Do you know, or can you guess, how these words originated?

The word **phoney** is given as having an unknown origin. What do you think its origin might have been? Discuss various possibilities and then make up your own dictionary entry for this word.

Invent a word of your own and write a complete dictionary entry for it. There is a checklist below to help you.

Try to make the word seem genuine: in other words give it a sound, a meaning, and an explanation which could belong to a real word. Who knows, it might catch on!

Headword	
Pronunciation	
Word class	
Definition	
Derivates	
Example	
Phrases	
Notes on usage	
Origin	

See if anyone can guess the meaning of your word. Tell them some of the details, but leave out the definition.

Oxford University Press

Walton Street Oxford OX2 6DP

Oxford   New York   Toronto
Delhi   Bombay   Calcutta   Madras   Karachi
Kuala Lumpur   Singapore   Hong Kong   Tokyo
Nairobi   Dar es Salaam   Cape Town
Melbourne   Auckland

and associated companies in
Berlin   Ibadan

Oxford is a trade mark of Oxford University Press

© Oxford University Press 1992

First published 1992

Redesigned impression 1994

10 9 8 7 6 5 4 3 2 1

All rights reserved. No part of this publication may be reproduced, stored in a retrieval system, or transmitted in any form or by any means, without the prior permission in writing of Oxford University Press. Within the UK, exceptions are allowed in respect of any fair dealing for the purpose of research or private study, or criticism or review, as permitted under the Copyright, Designs and Patents Act, 1988, or in the case of reprographic reproduction in accordance with the terms of licences issued by the Copyright Licensing Agency. Enquiries concerning reproduction outside those terms and in other countries should be sent to the Rights Department, Oxford University Press, at the address above.

This book is sold subject to the condition that it shall not, by way of trade or otherwise, be lent, re-sold, hired out, or otherwise circulated without the publisher's prior consent in any form of binding or cover other than that in which it is published and without a similar condition including this condition being imposed on the subsequent purchasers.

British Library Cataloguing in Publication Data
Data available

ISBN 0 19 910325 9 (paperback)

OWLS
OXFORD ENGLISH DICTIONARY WORD AND LANGUAGE SERVICE

Do you have a query about words, their origin, meaning, use, spelling, pronunciation, or any other aspect of the English language? Then write to OWLS at Oxford University Press, Walton Street, Oxford OX2 6DP.

All queries will by answered using the full resources of the Oxford Dictionary Department.

Printed and bound in Great Britain by
Butler & Tanner Ltd, Frome and London